The Way of Opulence

A 30 days devotional to attune you to wealth.

INTRODUCTION

In a world where the pursuit of abundance and fulfillment often leads to convoluted paths and contradictory advice, "The Way of Opulence" emerges as a guiding light, illuminating a transformative journey toward true prosperity. In this compelling volume, we embark on a voyage that transcends material wealth, delving into the profound wisdom underlying a life of opulence in all its facets – from financial prosperity and emotional well-being to spiritual richness. With each turn of the page, we unravel the secrets held by ancient masters, and timeless philosophies, all converging to reveal a holistic approach to abundance and success. Join us as we explore the intricate tapestry of desires, intentions, actions, and beliefs that weave together to create "The Way of Opulence." As you embark on this literary odyssey, prepare to recalibrate your understanding of prosperity and chart a course toward a life lived in fullness and opulence.

Foreword

These words are to be studied and savored daily over and over until their meaning deepens and flowers into the grace of Christ living in you and as you, allowing the ray of that Light to penetrate your mind, correcting every perception you have ever held about yourself or the world.

The 30 lessons contained in this volume reveal that the "Way" taught by Jeshua, and other great masters that graced the face of our planet and now presented to you so that the fulfillment of your desires becomes your everyday reality.

 May you be transformed by The Way of Opulence in your unique process of Living your day-to-day life.

Dedication

This book is dedicated to all the souls which hunger and thirst after Opulence; that they may have it; and have it abundantly.

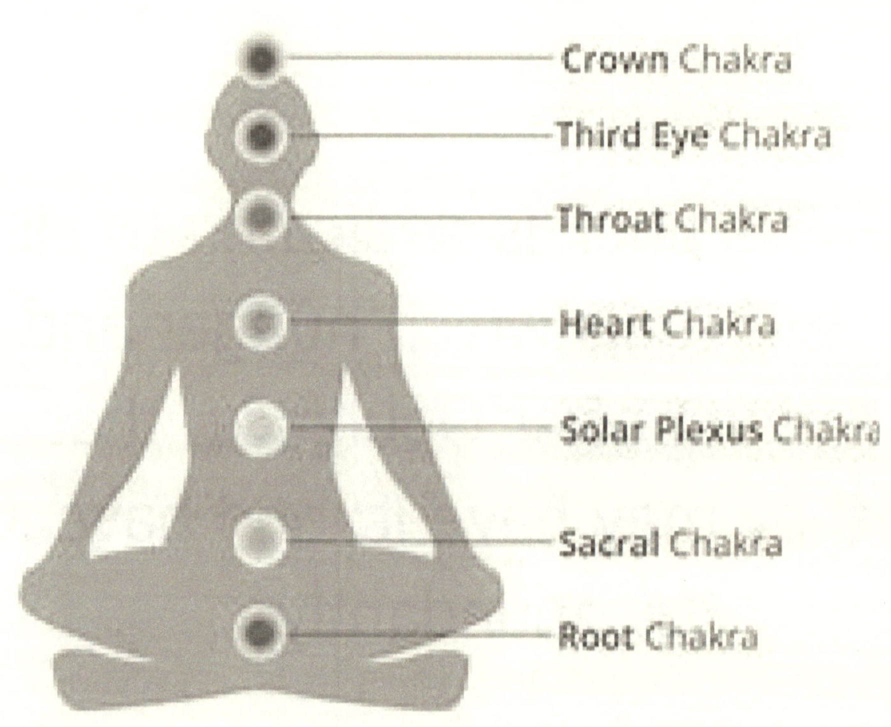

LOTUS POSITION

Thou Infinite, All-Pervading Presence! With Thy Mighty Radiance surging forth throughout the atmosphere of Earth, we give praise and thanks for

the onrushing Christ's Power of Love and Wisdom, which with certainty is raising the consciousness of mankind above the sordid selfishness of the activity of the outer self.

We give praise and thanks that we have become conscious of Thy Mighty, Active Presence at all times, and that in the conscious recognition of Thee, Thou dost charge our minds and bodies with Thy Pure Presence forever.

DAY ONE
THE WAY OF THE SPIRIT

1

Verse-"There is one body and one Spirit, one Lord, one faith, one baptism, one God and Father of all, who is over all and through all and in all." Ephesians 4:4

At the deepest level, everything in the universe is intrinsically connected and emerges from One source the "Spirit". This is the fundamental source of energy from which all manifestations arise. Spirit is an underlying essence that permeates all aspects of the universe, from the tiniest particle to the vast expanses of space. Spirit is not confined to a specific location or limited by physical boundaries. Spirit is an intelligent force that possesses infinite wisdom and creative abilities. It is the Universal Mind or Infinite Intelligence, the source of all creation and the driving force behind the manifestation of reality. The Spirit is not in itself physical or material, it throws out physical and material vehicles through which to function as its means of expression, in varying degrees of intelligence, such as plant, animal, and human. As it thinks of a form it takes that form, as it thinks of a motion it makes that motion. That is the way all things were created. Your mind is an individualized aspect of the great Universal Mind. It brought you into existence for self-expressing itself through you. Your mind draws its ability to think from the Universal mind and can also impress thoughts to the Universal mind. You can impress a thought on this Universal Mind and cause the thing you think to be acted upon by the One Spirit. Your repeated daily thoughts impressed on the Universal Mind have created the reality you currently identify with. Changing how you think daily is the starting point for a change in your reality.

LESSON 1 - THE SPIRIT POSSESSES THE ABILITY TO SHAPE AND INFLUENCE REALITY THROUGH ITS CREATIVE ENERGY.

PRAYER: GRACIOUS FATHER, AS I STAND AT THE THRESHOLD OF NEW OPPORTUNITIES AND CHALLENGES, I RECOGNIZE THE NEED FOR A DEEPER LEVEL OF FAITH. FILL ME WITH THE COURAGE TO STEP OUT IN FAITH, KNOWING THAT YOU ARE WITH ME EVERY STEP OF THE WAY.

MEDITATION

How to meditate

If you can master this art of meditation, your mental state will be such that you can use your imagination to solve problems.

However, for now, we will only focus on meditation; issue-solving will come later. With your feet flat on the floor, take a seat comfortably on a chair or a bed. Lay your hands down in your lap loosely. Sit cross-legged in the lotus pose if you'd like.

Hold your head upright and poised; avoid sagging. Now, deliberately relax each area of your body one at a time by concentrating on it first. Start with your left foot, move on to your left leg, right foot, right leg, and so forth until you reach your throat, face, eyes, and scalp. The first time you do this, you'll be shocked by how rigid your body was. Now choose a location on the ceiling or the wall opposite you that is about 45 degrees above eye level. If you are in an open space you can concentrate your gaze on the space between your eyes (third eye chakra). Look there until your eyelids start to drop, let them close. Now, slowly, at about two-second intervals, count backward from one hundred to one. As you do this, keep your mind on it, breathe deeply and you will be in Alpha state, for the very first time.

Morning Gratitude

Date: _______________________

Today I Learnt...

____
____
____

Today I will apply what I learned by...

____
____
____

3 things I'm grateful for today are...

____
____
____

"Happiness is a habit."

THE WAY OF CONSCIOUSNESS

2

Verse: "Nothing in all creation is hidden from God." - Hebrews 4:13

There is only One Consciousness in all the Universe, manifesting in legions of forms or levels of consciousness. This consciousness is the undifferentiated consciousness of the Father. Nothing exists outside of this One consciousness. We are all differentiated parts of this consciousness. If you could imagine a radio station that sends out different frequencies, e.g., 99.7, 97.8, 98.5, etc. Your brain only acts as a receiver of these frequencies and tunes into one, hence creating a personality (personal reality) for you. The reality you experience is the One consciousness experiencing it through you, in other words, you are one with this consciousness, but you are experiencing just a fragment of the whole. Consciousness is not of the physical dimension; it emanates from the source of all life (the Father), into the physical dimension. You experience only the effects of your consciousness, which is the conception of yourself. You may conceive yourself to be a rich or poor man and emanate that concept in the world, but the center of your being remains the same regardless of the concept you hold of yourself. It is only by a change of consciousness, that is by changing the concept you have of yourself (becoming someone else) that you can manifest (manifest; means experiencing the results of your conception in the world) your desires.

LESSON 2- NOTHING THAT YOU EXPERIENCE IS CAUSED BY ANYTHING OUTSIDE OF YOU.

P R A Y E R: SUPREME CREATOR WE THANK YOU FOR CREATING US AND GIVING US THE GIFT OF CONSCIOUSNESS. HELP US TO UNDERSTAND MORE ABOUT YOUR PLAN FOR OUR LIVES AND HOW WE CAN USE OUR CONSCIOUSNESS TO BRING GLORY TO YOUR NAME.

MEDITATION
Further Meditation

If all you do is learn to meditate, you will still be able to solve difficulties. In meditation, something lovely occurs, and the beauty you discover is soothing. The more you practice meditation, the more deeply you enter inside yourself and the more firmly you will hold onto an inner calm that nothing in life will be able to shatter.

If you feel that nothing happened during the previous exercise, it simply means you have been in Alpha many times before without being particularly aware of it. Simply relax, don't question it, and stay with the exercises.

Use the hundred-to-one method for ten mornings. Then count only from fifty to one, twenty-five to one, then ten to one, and finally five to one, ten mornings each.

To come out of the Alpha state, say these words "I will slowly come out as I count from one to five, feeling wide awake and better than before. It is in the Alpha state that problems are solved. Stick with the exercise until you can enter at will any moment of the day into the Alpha state.

Morning Gratitude

Date: _______________________

Today I Learnt...

____
____
____

Today I will apply what I learned by...

____
____
____

3 things I'm grateful for today are...

____
____
____

"Happiness is a habit."

THE WAY OF AWARENESS

3

Verse: "....I AM THAT I AM" Exodus 3:14

I AM is the self-definition of the absolute, the foundation on which everything exists. I AM is the self-definition of the Father. I AM is the feeling of permanent awareness, the very essence of consciousness. I may forget who I am, where I am, and what I am, but I cannot forget that I AM. Your awareness of being remains regardless of the forgetfulness of the concept you have of yourself. I AM is the Activity of Life. When you say and feel "I AM," you release the spring of Eternal, Everlasting Life to flow on Its way unmolested. In other words, you open wide the door to Its natural flow. When you say, "I AM not," you shut the door in the face of this Mighty Energy. "I AM" is the Full Activity of God. The first expression every Self-conscious form of Life gives is "I AM." It is only afterward, in its contact with outer, wrongly qualified activity, that it begins to accept anything less than "I AM. When you say "I AM sick," or "I AM broke" it is an abject falsehood in respect to your Divinity, which cannot be sick or in lack. Continually remind yourself, "I AM which is all health and opulence". You are, in a relationship with all created things, and there is communication that occurs without ceasing, but you have selected out aspects of creation to focus your attention on, hence creating your limited awareness. You are, therefore, never experiencing anything except what you have chosen to create through your selection of events that you have dropped, like pebbles into the pool of your awareness. Expanding your awareness can lead to greater self-realization and the ability to consciously shape your life.

LESSON 3 - I AM THE ONE WHO CHOOSES THE EFFECTS I EXPERIENCE.

PRAYER: HEAVENLY FATHER, GRANT ME THE WISDOM TO SEE BEYOND THE LIMITATIONS OF MY CURRENT AWARENESS. HELP ME EMBRACE THE TRANSFORMATIVE POWER OF SHIFTING MY AWARENESS TO ALIGN WITH DIVINE TRUTH AND ABUNDANCE.

Yoga Practice
The Mountain Pose

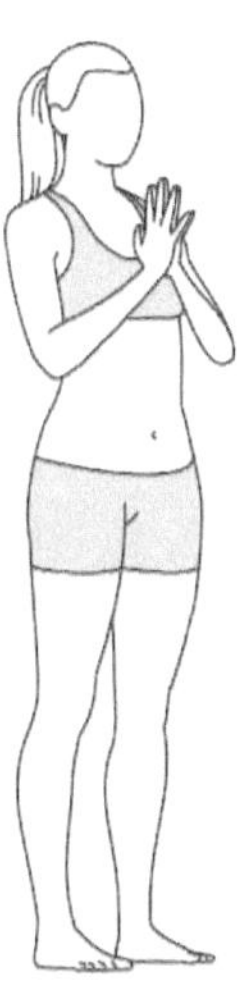

How to do it

Stand up tall with your feet together, your spine long, and your body relaxed. Bring your palms together in front of the heart. Stay for 30 seconds to 1 minute.

Distribute your weight equally between both feet, breathe easily, close your eyes, and feel the energy flowing through your body.

The benefits

The mountain pose helps to improve posture, strengthens the legs, thighs, knees, and ankles, and firms the abdomen.

Morning Gratitude

Date: _______________________

Today I Learnt...

____
____
____

Today I will apply what I learned by...

____
____
____

3 things I'm grateful for today are...

____
____
____

"Happiness is a habit."

THE WAY OF MINDFULNESS

4

Verse: - "Do not conform to the pattern of this world, but be transformed by the renewing of your mind." Romans 12:2

In today's fast-paced world, it's easy to get caught up in the hustle and bustle of life and forget about the importance of being mindful. Mindfulness is a practice that helps you to slow down and focus on the present moment. It allows you to become more aware of your thoughts, feelings, and surroundings, which can lead to a greater sense of peace and contentment. No matter what happens during the day, turn within and be still. Know that you share in the same Consciousness with the Father and all things are possible to you. The mind is the seat of consciousness. It is where your thoughts and emotions originate. You ought to renew your mind daily with truths that align your thoughts with the Creator. The world moves with motiveless necessity. This simply means it has no motive of its own, but it's under the necessity of manifesting your concept. You are imprisoned by the present concept of yourself. To free yourself you must rearrange the structure of your mind. There is only One mind, in all the universe, what differs is the arrangement of the thought patterns in your mind. However, your mind is always arranged in the pattern of all you believe and consent to as true. Henceforth you should be intentional about what you allow into your mind. Fill your minds with things that are pure, lovely, and of good report; things you want to see manifest in your life.

LESSON 4- HEALTH, WEALTH, BEAUTY, AND GENIUS ARE NOT CREATED. THEY ARE MANIFESTED BY THE CONTENTS OF YOUR MIND.

PRAYER: HEAVENLY FATHER, HELP US TO BE MORE MINDFUL OF YOUR PRESENCE IN OUR LIVES. TEACH US TO BE STILL AND FOCUS ON THE PRESENT MOMENT, SO WE CAN EXPERIENCE YOUR PEACE AND JOY.

Yoga Practice
The Tree-pose

How to do it

Find a fixed point in front of you and stare at it to help you balance.

As you inhale, shift the weight into your left foot and lift your right foot an inch off the floor. Bring the foot to your shin or inner thigh using your right hand. Avoid placing your foot directly on the knee.

As you exhale, ground through the standing leg and lengthen through the crown of your head. Bring your palms to touch above your head into prayer hands.

The benefits

This pose helps improve concentration and your ability to balance by strengthening the arches of the feet and the outer hips.

Morning Gratitude

Date: _______________________

Today I want to Achieve...

____
____
____

Today I will be Mindful by...

____
____
____

3 things I'm grateful for today are...

____
____
____

"Happiness is a habit."

THE WAY OF THE FATHER

5

Verse- "I and My Father are one." John 10:30

Everything in this world is a state of consciousness pushed out and is contained within the Father. The opening verse states "I and my father are one. If you read further, it defines the relationship with the Father, by stating "But my Father who sent me is greater than I, so I go to my Father". This means, although you share in the One consciousness of the Creator, He sent you into the material world, to experience all of His creation through you. Therefore, the "I" which is your exterior persona is inferior to your essential consciousness the Sender, and must live by faith in the Father. The Father resides in the very depth of your being, He knows your every thought and your desire, for there is no secret you can keep from your very being, hence there is no separation between you and the Father. "If we know that He hears us in whatever we ask, we know that we already possess what we have asked of Him*(1 John 5:15)*." The manifestation of your desire is entirely measured by your capacity to know that the life and power in you is the same life and power which brought you into existence. You succeeded in manifesting a couple of times, without understanding the power, because you used it unconsciously, and according to the Law of its nature, you reached harmonious results. Your ability at all times to use this power unfailingly depends upon your conscious recognition of its presence. "For he that cometh to God must believe that He exists and that He is a rewarder of them that earnestly seek Him*(Hebrew 11:6)*."

LESSON 5- THE FATHER IS THE I AM OF MAN. HE TOOK UPON THE PERSONA YOU ARE IDENTIFIED WITH TODAY.

PRAYER: OUR FATHER WHO ART IN HEAVEN, HALLOWED BE THY NAME, THY KINGDOM COME. THY WILL BE DONE ON EARTH AS IT IS IN HEAVEN. GIVE US THIS DAY OUR DAILY BREAD, AND FORGIVE US OUR TRESPASSES, AS WE FORGIVE THOSE WHO TRESPASS AGAINST US,

Yoga Practice
The chair pose

How to do it

Start in Mountain Pose. As you inhale, raise your arms, spread your fingers, and reach up through your fingertips. As you exhale, sit back and down as if sitting in a chair. Hold this position for a while.

Shift your weight toward the heels and lengthen up through the spine. As you inhale, stand and lengthen through your arms. As you exhale, sit deeper into the pose.

The benefits

The sitting and standing pose (give it a minute, you'll feel the burn) strengthens your legs, upper back, and shoulders. As a bonus, you'll have an opportunity to practice patience as your thighs work hard. Just remember to breathe.

Morning Gratitude

Date: ________________________

Today I want to Achieve...

____
____
____

Today I will improve my awareness by...

____
____
____

3 things I'm grateful for today are...

____
____
____

"Happiness is a habit."

THE WAY OF THE SUBCONSCIOUS

6

Verse-"But we have this treasure in earthen vessels, that the excellency of the power may be of God, and not of us.?" 2 Corinthians 4:7

The subconscious is the most important part of consciousness. It is the realm of cause while the conscious mind is the realm of effect. The subconscious is what a man *is*, while the conscious is what a man *Knows*. The conscious and the subconscious are one consciousness, but the subconscious is greater than the conscious. "I and my father are one, but the father is greater than me". Your objective conscious mind of itself has only *Will*, it is the subconscious that provides the *Power*. When the conscious and the subconscious mind are in harmony, you have *Willpower*.

The subconscious is that in which everything is known, to which everything is possible, from which everything comes, and to which everything goes. You perceive your current reality with your conscious mind via the five senses, it then transmits your thoughts and belief of what you perceive as true, to the subconscious while you sleep, which in turn objectifies your belief in your conscious reality. By feeding your subconscious mind with positive and harmonious thoughts, you create corresponding circumstances and events in your life. The subconscious mind operates based on the dominant thoughts and beliefs you hold. It does not differentiate between what is real or imagined, good or bad, but instead accepts and acts upon the instructions it receives from your conscious mind. The subconscious mind works incessantly to bring your predominant thoughts into physical reality.

LESSON 6- THE SUBCONSCIOUS MIND IS NOT LOGICAL; IT ONLY UNDERSTANDS AND COMMUNICATES THROUGH FEELINGS AND EMOTIONS.

PRAYER: FATHER, I PRAY THAT YOU WOULD REPLACE ANY NEGATIVE OR HARMFUL BELIEFS STORED IN MY SUBCONSCIOUS WITH YOUR WORD AND YOUR PROMISES. HELP ME TO UPROOT ANY LIES, FEARS, OR DOUBTS THAT HAVE TAKEN ROOT DEEP WITHIN ME.

Yoga Practice
Seated Forward Fold

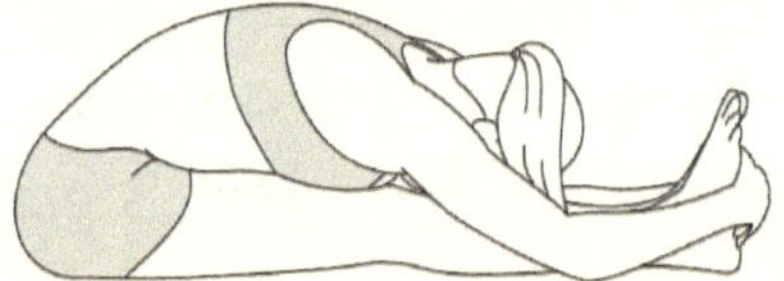

How to do it

Sit and straighten your legs out in front of you, grounding your thighs into the floor. Hinge at the hips to elongate your torso over your thighs.

Grab hold of the outer edges of your feet.

You can also sit on the edge of a blanket to help you fold forward

The benefit

This improves blood flow to your spine and stretches your hamstrings.

Morning Gratitude

Date: _______________

Today I want to Achieve...

____
____
____

Today I will improve my awareness by...

____
____
____

3 things I'm grateful for today are...

____
____
____

"Happiness is a habit."

THE WAY OF DESIRE

7

Verse: - "Delight yourself in the Lord, and he will give you the desires of your heart." Psalm 37:4

Desire is everything. It is that energy that brings forth all waves of creation out of the depth of the Creator.

In truth, you do not lift the body from your couch to the refrigerator without the desire to eat. Therefore, desire is not to be feared for it is not evil as you have been told, rather it is to be mastered. Mastery of desire comes when you recognize that you are safe to feel whatever wave of desire might come up through your consciousness because you decide whether or not you will bring it into manifestation. For if you are to ever create as the Father creates, you will need to heal your conflicted perceptions about desire, you will need to transcend the energy of fear.

It is because of this fear most people don't know what they truly desire, that is they don't want what they are trying to manifest. To be sure of your desire, your mind, body, and spirit must agree with what you are trying to manifest. If there is any resistance from any part of your being, then you will not manifest for "two cannot walk together except they agree". If perhaps what you are trying to manifest seems too big or is too much of a leap, you can tune it down and check how you truly feel about it. You must believe strongly that your desire is achievable, this will strengthen your faith in the Father and give you the resolve to attain it. Your heart-felt desire will manifest in ways you did not think possible.

LESSON 7- DESIRE IS CREATION; WHAT YOU DECREE IS, AND THE THOUGHTS YOU HOLD IN YOUR MIND WILL BE REFLECTED THROUGH THE NATURE OF YOUR EXPERIENCE.

PRAYER: SUPREME CREATOR AS I PURSUE MY DESIRES, I ASK FOR YOUR STRENGTH AND PERSEVERANCE. EMPOWER ME TO OVERCOME OBSTACLES AND SETBACKS THAT MAY COME MY WAY.

SELF EXERCISE

An Exercise On Desire

For just ten or fifteen minutes, set aside your world.

Relax the body and close your eyes. It can be of great benefit to let the breath become very deep and rhythmic. It relaxes the nervous system. As

you relax the body and the mind, ask yourself:

What do I truly want?

Observe the images that come, without judgment. Notice the feelings in the body and allow this to go on for just a minute or two. Then pause, open your eyes, and write down all that you can remember. For example, "I saw the image of having golden coins rain down upon me so that I had to have an umbrella over my head. I saw huge bowls of ice cream. Whatever it is, write it down.

Then, take a deep breath, relax again, and repeat the process.

Do this over a period of ten or fifteen minutes so that you repeat the process at least six or seven times, writing everything down.

When you have done this seven times, so that you have seven sheets of paper in which you have gone through this process, then, and only then,

begin to look back through all the things that came up. Ask yourself, "What seems to be repeating itself?" The desire with the most repetition is what you truly want and should be given your full attention if you are to create it in the field of your reality.

Morning Gratitude

Date: ___________________

What do I truly desire...

How will attaining my desire make me feel...

3 things I'm grateful for today are...

"Happiness is a habit."

THE WAY OF VIBRATION

8

Verse- "and all the things reproved by the light are manifested, for everything that is manifested is light." Ephesians 5:13

All of creation is made of energy and all things of energy translate into light. A person, a feeling, a thing, a color, words even your thought; at its core level is a vibrating light wave.

Our thoughts and feelings also create forms that are made of vibrating light waves. They may not become concrete matter in your reality immediately, but the energy is still out there in the universe. The events that occur in your life are all light waves vibrating in the unified space of One universal mind. Nothing is truly at rest in the universe everything vibrates, everything moves. The difference between the various manifestations in the universe is due to the varying degree of vibration by every light wave. Matter and spirit are but different degrees of vibration. All matter can be described in terms of its vibration, whether an object is hot or cold depends on the degree of vibration of its electrons.

Opulence and lack are on the same scale but of different degrees of vibration, in the thought pattern of man. Man is always in a state of constant vibration, it is this state that determines the events which unfold in his day-to-day activities.

Vibration produces energy and this energy is measured using frequency. High frequency signifies a high energy level, low frequency means a low energy level.

LESSON 8- ALL MANIFESTATIONS OF THOUGHT, EMOTION, OR ANY MENTAL STATE ARE ACCOMPANIED BY VIBRATION.

PRAYER: LOVING FATHER, I INVITE YOU TO EXPAND MY HEART AND REVEAL THE INFINITE POSSIBILITIES THAT LIE BEFORE ME. HELP ME TO SEE BEYOND THE LIMITATIONS OF MY CURRENT CIRCUMSTANCES AND ACCESS THE REALMS OF DIVINE INSPIRATION.

Yoga Practice
The Downward Dog Pose

How to do it

From all fours, walk your hands 6 inches in front of you. Tuck your toes and lift your hips up and back to lengthen your spine. If your hamstrings are tight, keep your knees bent to bring your weight back into the legs.

Spread your fingers wide, press into your hands, and rotate your arms so that your biceps are facing toward one another. Press your thighs back toward the wall behind you.

The benefits

This classic pose opens your shoulders, lengthens your spine, and stretches your hamstrings. Since your head is below your heart, the mild inversion creates a calming effect.

Morning Gratitude

Date: ______________________

Today learnt .. .

____
____
____

TodayIwill improve my self by...

____
____
____

3 things I'm grateful for today are...

____
____
____

"Happiness is a habit."

THE WAY OF FREQUENCY

9

**Verse- "Since, then, you have been raised with Christ, set your hearts on things above."
Colossians 3:1**

Everything in the universe has a signature frequency of the Divine force, which flows through it. High frequencies carry more divine energy, Low frequencies carry less divine energy.

Frequencies affect what happens in your life. You create your life with your frequency choices. This is called frequency attunement. Frequency attunement works under the Law of Sympathetic Resonance, which states that; Two things that have the same frequency, will form a connection and resonate with each other in harmony. Light waves that vibrate with the same frequency will be drawn together. Therefore, you will draw things to your life that reflect the frequency of your being.

You are designing your life at every moment. You are either consciously choosing frequencies, or you are unconsciously choosing them.

Worry is a low frequency you need to let go of. Fear, and anxiety all have less of the divine energy and should be removed from your thought. Faith in the Father is high frequency and it pulls your desire easily to you.

To create the life you want, your job is to get out of the low frequency of fear and find a way back into the high frequency of faith and gratitude. Always speak words of encouragement to yourself and others around you. Listen to music and conversation that takes you to a high frequency of joy and gratitude, this way your life will attract everything with a similar frequency.

LESSON 9- YOU MAKE THE CHOICES THAT CREATE YOUR LIFE. UNDERSTANDING FREQUENCY WILL EMPOWER YOU TO CREATE THE LIFE OF YOUR DREAMS.

PRAYER: LOVING FATHER, MAY MY VISIONS AND DREAMS BE IN HARMONIOUS SYNCHRONY WITH YOUR LOVING PLANS FOR MY LIFE AND THE WORLD AROUND ME TODAY,

Yoga Practice
Staff Pose

How to do it

Start in Downward-Facing Dog. Shift forward so your shoulders are stacked over your wrists. Draw your navel in toward your spine and keep your hips from dropping.

Reach heels back as you lengthen the crown of your head forward. Ground down into hands, pushing the floor away beneath you. Lengthen through the arms and broaden your chest.

The benefit

Considered one of the best moves for core strength, plank pose strengthens your abdominals and promotes stability.

Morning Gratitude

Date: _______________

Today I want to Achieve...

____

____

____

Today I will improve my self by...

____

____

____

3 things I'm grateful for today are...

____

____

____

"Happiness is a habit."

THE WAY OF THOUGHT
10

Verse-, "For as he thinketh in his heart so is he". Proverbs 23:7

Thought is the way by which you can communicate your desires to the One Spirit or the Father within you. The one Spirit which created all things and permeates all space and existence is a thinking and intelligent power. The One Spirit moves according to its thoughts. Everything you see in nature is the visible expression of a thought in the One Spirit or One Mind. You are a thinking center and can originate thoughts. If you can form a thing desired in your thoughts and steadily impress your thought upon the One Mind, your desire will be fulfilled. It is rare to find anyone who will admit that the cause of his failure or continued misfortune lies within himself. This is because almost all individuals lack the understanding that a certain quality of thought will bring to their consciousness, a recognition of an intelligent power capable of attracting to them, the fulfillment of their purpose and the attainment of their desire. Your job is to use your power of thought and feeling to attain positive results. Use it negatively, and you get negative results. Every person has the natural and inherent power to think whatever he wants, but it requires more effort to think positive thoughts in the face of negative circumstances. To think of truth regardless of appearance is laborious and will require practice. The person living the life he desires has consciously gained mastery of his thoughts.

LESSON 10- YOU ARE A THINKING CENTER AND CAN ORIGINATE THOUGHTS. CONSCIOUS USE OF THIS THOUGHTS MAKES TREMENDOUS POWER AVAILABLE TO YOU

PRAYER: GRACIOUS FATHER, GUIDE US IN UNDERSTANDING THE CREATIVE FORCE WITHIN OUR THOUGHTS. HELP US TO ALIGN OUR THOUGHTS WITH YOUR TRUTH AND USE OUR MINDS TO BRING FORTH POSITIVE CHANGE IN OUR LIVES AND THE LIVES OF OTHERS.

Yoga Practice
Plank Pose

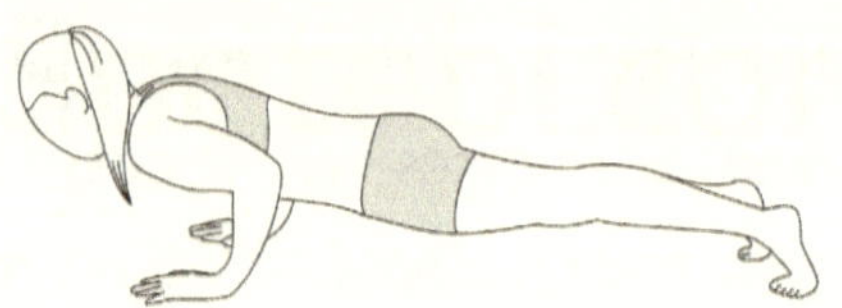

How to do it

From Staff Pose, shift forward onto your tippy toes. Ground through your palms and broaden across the chest. Take an inhale.

On an exhale, bend your elbows to a 90-degree angle. Keep your thighs lifted toward the ceiling. Imagine stretching your tailbone toward your heels as you lengthen through the spine. Hold your elbows in line with the torso. Gaze forward.

To come out of the pose, release your knees to the ground. You can also keep your knees lifted and lower down onto your stomach for an extra ab challenge. Another option is to lift up and back to a Downward-Facing Dog and relax.

The benefit

This is a key part of Sun Salutations, which you'll find in Hatha, Sivananda, Ashtanga, and Vinyasa yoga classes. It promotes core stability and strengthens your abdominals and triceps.

Morning Gratitude

Date: _______________

What doialwa ys think about   ...

Toda y I w ill f ocus m y thought on ...

3 things I'm grateful for today are...

"Happiness is a habit."

THE WAY OF WORDS
11

Verse-; " the worlds were framed by the word of God so that things which are seen were not made of things which do appear." Hebrew 11:3

The world was created through spoken words. The very act of speaking brought forth existence. Similarly, your words possess the power to create and shape your reality. Two things add power to the words you use: your level of mind, and your degree of emotional involvement with what you say. By aligning your words with higher truths, you participate in the ongoing process of creation and shaping your reality in collaboration with the One Consciousness. The word is not just a sound or a written symbol. The word is a force; it is the power you have to express and communicate, to think and thereby create the events in your life. What other creature on earth can speak? The word is the most powerful tool you have as a human. But like a sword with two edges, your words can create the most beautiful life or destroy everything around you. Be impeccable with your words, that is do not use your words against yourself or someone else. Words are seeds that are planted into the soil of the human mind. When a person accepts the words uttered to him as truth, they germinate and produce good or terrible fruits based on what was said. We dull our appetite for a good life with negative words, and these words, gathering power with repetition, create negative outcomes in our lives. Your words and your thoughts must be in harmony. You cannot think of acquiring wealth while at the same time complain about lack. Your words must reflect your new state of belief about yourself. Speak kind and encouraging words to yourself and others.

LESSON 11- OUR WORDS CAN EITHER MAKE OR BREAK US. FOR LIFE AND DEATH ARE IN THE POWER OF THE TONGUE.

PRAYER: TEACH ME, LORD, TO BE MINDFUL OF THE WORDS I SPEAK IN MOMENTS OF FRUSTRATION OR ANGER. GRANT ME SELF-CONTROL AND PATIENCE, SO THAT I MAY CHOOSE MY WORDS WISELY AND REFRAIN FROM CAUSING UNNECESSARY HURT OR DIVISION.

AFFIRMATION

I AM attracting unlimited financial abundance and opportunities I into my life, effortlessly and joyfully.

I AM the fulfillment and sustaining of everything I desire.

I AM the source of Wealth inside, which expresses Itself in my inner and outer self.

I AM the source that vibrates and aligns with Abundance.

I AM part of this Abundant and Prosperous world and for this I allow myself to be Grateful for the great wealth that I AM enjoying in Abundance today.

Morning Gratitude

Date: _______________

Today le arnt …

____

____

____

Today lw i ll imp rove m yse lf by......

____

____

____

3 things I'm grateful for today are...

____

____

____

"Happiness is a habit."

THE WAY OF IMAGINATION

12

Verse- "Now to him who is able to do immeasurably more than all we ask or imagine, according to His power that is at work within us." Ephesians 3:20

Imagination is the way to successfully impress your thought on Universal Mind. It is the key to unlocking your creative potential and transforming your life. Your outer world is a reflection of your inner world, your imagination plays a central role in creating this inner world. Everything you see in the external world was first conceived in the realm of imagination. Imagination is the redeeming power in man. This is the power spoken of in the opening verse. An awakened imagination works with a goal in mind. It generates and preserves the desirable while transforming or destroying the undesirable. To the unenlightened, this will all appear to be fantasy, but all progress comes from individuals who do not accept the established view or the world as it is.

If you judge after appearances, you will continue to be enslaved by the evidence of your senses. To cultivate the faculty of imagination, you should deliberately disentangle your mind from the evidence of the senses and focus your attention on an invisible state, mentally feeling it and sensing it until it has all the distinctness of reality. Earnest, concentrated thought focused on a particular direction shuts out other sensations and causes them to disappear. A little practice will convince you that you can, by controlling your imagination, reshape your future in harmony with your desire. Imagine with the place of the wished fulfilled, what would be experienced in the flesh, were you to achieve your goal; and you shall, in time meet in the flesh as you met it in your imagination.

LESSON 12 -WHATEVER WE CAN IMAGINE VIVIDLY AND PERSISTENTLY, WE HAVE THE POTENTIAL TO BRING INTO EXISTENCE

PRAYER: STRENGTHEN OUR FAITH IN THE POWER OF IMAGINATION. HELP US TO BELIEVE IN THE VISIONS AND DREAMS YOU HAVE PLACED WITHIN OUR HEARTS. MAY OUR IMAGINATION BE FUELED BY UNWAVERING FAITH IN YOU.

IMAGINATION PRACTICE

First, begin by entering into the Alpha state as described in the meditation technique on day one of this book. After you have successfully entered this state proceed with the following steps:

1. Selecting a goal: Choose a specific goal or desire that you want to manifest. It could be related to various aspects of life, such as health, relationships, career, or abundance.

2. Creating a mental image: Close your eyes and visualize the desired outcome as vividly as possible. See yourself already in possession of what you desire. Engage all your senses to make the mental image as real as you can, incorporating the sounds, smells, textures, and emotions associated with your goal.

3. Repetition and belief: Repeat the visualization exercise regularly, ideally just before falling asleep and upon waking up. This will cultivate a deep belief that the desired outcome is already a reality. This conviction strengthens the power of visualization.

4. Detachment and gratitude: After visualizing, detach from the outcome and trust in the process. Avoid obsessing over the how and when of manifestation. Express gratitude for the manifestation of your desire, as if it has already been fulfilled.

Morning Gratitude

Date: _______________

What do i truly Desire...

____

____

____

Three Scenarios From my Imagination

____

____

____

3 things I'm grateful for today are...

____

____

____

"Happiness is a habit."

THE WAY OF ASSUMPTION

13

Verse- "Now faith is the substance of things hoped for, the evidence of things not seen."
Hebrew 11:1

Your assumptions about yourself, run your life. In simple terms, your life manifests through your persistent assumptions. This all happens so naturally that you will not believe it. It is one of the greatest illusions of this life. Your consistent and persistent assumptions about yourself, so naturally picture itself in the world that you will say it would have happened anyway. You will give credit to the series of events that brought about the assumption into being, as you will be oblivious to your assumption being the real cause of the phenomenon. For assumptions about yourself to materialize, it must be deeply rooted in a sense of belief. For instance, even if you pretend to be a lion for an entire year, you won't change into one, because you already know that's not possible. However, if you are poor, you can continue to assume you are wealthy since you are aware that a poor person can become wealthy, if you continue to assume the feeling of your wish is fulfilled and continue feeling that it is fulfilled until that which you feel objectifies itself. You will become wealthy. The worse off a man is, the worse it gets for him, simply because he is probably assuming the worst to come in his life and so it is. Similarly, if you begin to assume the good and accept all your desires, if you feel worthy of them and encourage them in your mind you will have them.

LESSON 13- THE INTERNAL CONVERSATIONS YOU HAVE WITH YOURSELF, THAT IS YOUR ASSUMPTIONS, SHAPE YOUR WORLD, THEREFORE HAVE GOOD INTERNAL CONVERSATIONS ABOUT YOUR LIFE.

PRAYER: GRACIOUS FATHER, AS I STAND AT THE THRESHOLD OF NEW OPPORTUNITIES AND CHALLENGES, I RECOGNIZE THE NEED FOR A DEEPER LEVEL OF FAITH. FILL ME WITH THE COURAGE TO STEP OUT IN FAITH, KNOWING THAT YOU ARE WITH ME EVERY STEP OF THE WAY.

Yoga Practice
Upward-Facing Dog

How to do it

Lie facedown on the floor. Bend elbows and place hands on the mat in line with lower ribs. Hug your elbows in line with your torso. Tuck your toes and take an inhale.

As you exhale, push the floor away like a push-up. Straighten your arms and broaden across the chest, hovering your hips a few inches above the floor at the same time

The benefits

You'll open up your chest and shoulders, while stretching the abdominals and hip flexors. This pose comes after chaturanga in a classic Sun Salutation

Morning Gratitude

Date: _______________________

What is my main goal...

____
____
____

New assu mp tions ab out m yse lf...

____
____
____

3 things I'm grateful for today are...

____
____
____

"Happiness is a habit."

DAY FOURTEEN

THE WAY OF OPPOSITES

14

Verse- "What, then, shall we say in response to these things? If God is for us, who can be against us?" Romans 8:31

Everything is dual, everything has an opposite; opposites are identical in nature but different in degree. There is a fundamental principle that states, "In the Absence of That Which You Are Not, That Which You are is Not." For instance, in the absence of COLD, HOT is not. Hot can be experienced as an idea, but not as a physical reality unless cold exists. Here is another illustration; if you have a mental image of yourself as six feet tall, that image will always be just that–a mental image. You can only experience being six feet tall in the physical world if there is another person around who is anything but six feet tall. In this case, you only perceive being six feet tall in relation to the other person who is the opposite of six feet tall. If everyone and everything in the world is six feet tall, you cannot know in your experience what six feet tall is, you can only have an idea. Hence for you to experience the idea of six-feet tallness, you will subconsciously beg the universe to send you anything opposite of six-feet tallness. The same thing happens when you ask or try to manifest an experience or an event in your life, everything opposite to that which you are trying to manifest must come first before the experience or the event you asked for will manifest. In this regard when you start seeing the contrast of your visualization begin to manifest, persist in your assumption and count it all joy for what you wished for is about to become a reality.

LESSON 14- "IN THE ABSENCE OF THAT WHICH YOU ARE NOT, THAT WHICH YOU ARE IS NOT."

PRAYER: WITH UNWAVERING FAITH, I STEP FORWARD INTO THE REALM OF INFINITE POSSIBILITIES. I AM OPEN TO RECEIVING YOUR DIVINE GUIDANCE AND BLESSINGS. AND SO IT IS.

Yoga Practice
The Bow Pose

How to do it

Lie facedown, roll your shoulder blades down the back, and send your arms back behind you. Bend your knees so that your feet are near your rare.

On an inhale, lift your upper body and legs off the floor, keeping the hips grounded. Reach back to grab outer ankles. Use the leverage to lift your body up and broaden across the chest.

The benefits

You'll open up your chest and shoulders, while stretching the abdominals and hip flexors. This pose comes after chaturanga in a classic Sun Salutation

Morning Gratitude

Date: _______________________

What is my main goal...

____

____

____

New assu mp tions ab out m yse lf ...

____

____

____

3 things I'm grateful for today are...

____

____

____

"Happiness is a habit."

THE WAY OF PERSISTENCE

15

Verse- " ...yet because of the man's persistence, he will get up and give him as much as he needs."
Luke 11:8

Persistence in a thought pattern regardless of external circumstances can alter your reality. Your external experiences can be influenced and molded by your thoughts and beliefs. Consistent thoughts and beliefs can assist you draw similar situations, events, and results into your life even when contradictory circumstances are present. If you are to achieve your desire, you must persevere in the feeling of the wish fulfilled every hour of every day. Persistently focusing your thoughts and attention on the desired outcome, or "Live in the End". This continuous focus creates a strong vibrational frequency associated with the desired outcome. Persistence in a thought pattern often involves maintaining a consistent emotional state aligned with the desired reality. Emotions serve as a powerful magnetic field that influences the vibrations we emit into the world. By persistently generating positive emotions, such as joy, gratitude, and excitement, you align yourselves with the reality you wish to manifest. You must be persistent in attaining your desire. Continue to imagine what you want until you have actually obtained it. You do nothing else to obtain your desire. If it is necessary to take some action, you will be led to do so in a normal, natural manner. You do not have to do anything to "help" bring it about. When you persistently hold a specific belief or expectation, your mind filters incoming information and selectively focuses on aspects that conform to your beliefs. This altered perception can then guide your actions and decisions in ways that align with your desired reality.

LESSON 15- CIRCUMSTANCES DON'T MATTER PERSIST IN YOUR ASSUMPTION AND YOU SHALL HAVE YOUR DESIRES.

PRAYER: FATHER, PLEASE GRANT ME THE WISDOM TO DISCERN WHEN TO PERSIST AND WHEN TO ADJUST MY COURSE. HELP ME TO LEARN FROM FAILURES AND SETBACKS, USING THEM AS STEPPING STONES TOWARDS GREATER SUCCESS

Yoga Practice
The Warrior Pose I

How to do it

Start in Downward-Facing Dog. Step one foot forward between your hands. Turn your back foot out, approximately 45 degrees, and ground down into your back foot.

Line your feet up heel to heel, or slightly wider. Bend the front knee directly over the front ankle while you straighten your back leg. Draw your back heel down toward the floor.

On an inhale, lengthen through the spine and lift your arms up. Place your hands on your hips or lift them up in a V toward the ceiling. Rotate your torso toward the front of the room.

The benefits

This energizing pose strengthens your legs, arms, and back muscles. It also gives your chest, shoulders, neck, thighs, and ankles a nice stretch.

Morning Gratitude

Date: _______________

What is my main goal...

____

____

____

New a s sum ptio ns abou t mys elf...

____

____

____

3 things I'm grateful for today are...

____

____

____

"Happiness is a habit."

THE WAY OF REPENTANCE

16

Verse- "Repent, then, and turn to God, so that your sins may be wiped out". Act 3:19

The word "Repentance" is gotten from the Greek word "Metanoia", which simply means; A fundamental transformation in the outlook of a man's vision of the world and himself. The word Sin on the other hand is translated from the Greek word "Hamartia", which means to miss the mark or to fail. If you have a goal and you have failed to achieve it, you have sinned. The word "Repent" can be divided into two; "Re" and "Pent". Re can mean to go back while "Pent" can be used to mean something at the top, like a Penthouse, therefore repentance can also mean going back to the top. The Bible made it known that man fell from glory because of sin, this means you were in a state of higher consciousness but because you failed to achieve a certain desire, you fell from that state of consciousness to a lower one. Therefore, man is called to repentance, to change the way he views reality and return to his previous consciousness in the Father. If you are unemployed but desire to be gainfully employed, you are in a lower state of consciousness, a state of unemployment, which is your current sin. To repent is to enact a scene in your imagination where you are gainfully employed to the degree that you are self-persuaded in your consciousness that you are what you imagined yourself to be and persistently dwell in that state of consciousness. This is how your "SIN" which is unemployment will be wiped out. For life makes no mistakes and always gives a man that which man first gives himself.

LESSON 16- CHANGE THE WAY YOU VIEW EVENTS HAPPENING IN YOUR LIFE. STOP PLAYING THE VICTIM, START ACTING AS THE CAUSE.

PRAYER: LORD, I REPENT FROM MY SINS OF FAILING TO ACHIEVE MY GOAL. I RECOGNIZE THAT WITH YOU ALL THINGS ARE POSSIBLE. I ASK FOR YOUR FORGIVENESS AND I LOOK UNTO YOU AS THE SOURCE OF MY SUPPLY.

Yoga Practice
The Warrior Pose II

How to do it

Stand with feet wide, 3–4 feet apart. Shift your right heel out so your toes are pointing slightly inward. Turn your left foot out 90 degrees. Line up your left heel with the arch of your right foot.

Bend your left knee to a 90-degree angle, keeping the knee in line with the second toe to protect the knee joint. Stretch through your straight back leg and ground down into the back foot.

On an inhale, bring arms to a T at shoulder height. Draw your shoulder blades down the back. Spread your fingers and keep your palms facedown. Gaze over the front fingers. As you exhale, sink deeper into the stretch.

The benefits

A pose with "warrior" in its name may not sound very zen, but this standing pose can help calm and steady your mind. Tougher than it looks, it also strengthens your legs and ankles while increasing stamina.

Morning Gratitude

Date: _______________________

What is my main goal...

____

____

____

New a s sum ptio ns abou t mys elf...

____

____

____

3 things I'm grateful for today are...

____

____

____

"Happiness is a habit."

DAY SEVENTEEN
THE WAY OF NOW

17

Verse-"behold, now is the accepted time; behold, now is the day of salvation". 2 Corinthians 6:2

Nothing can exist outside of the now, the present moment. Nothing ever happens in the past and nothing will ever happen in the future, all is happening in the NOW. What you think of as the past is a memory trace, stored in the mind of a former now. When you remember the past, you activate the memory trace and you do so NOW. The future is an imagined NOW, a projection of the mind. When the future comes it comes in the NOW. Past and future have no reality of their own, because when you think of them you do it in the NOW. When you want to achieve a goal by visualizing, you should not visualize achieving the goal in the future, because there is no future, you must visualize achieving it NOW. You must have the fullness of joy in the present moment of your desired goal achieved. For example, if your goal is to sell millions of copies of your book to people, you imagine a scene of your book in the hands of millions of people, not in the future but in the present moment. Feel what it feels like to have sold that many copies and you merge that vision with the fullness of life and joy in the present moment. Do not wait for the manifestation to happen before you can feel the joy, feel it in the NOW. The present moment is the key to all achievement. It is all you ever have, there is never a time when your life is not in "The Now".

LESSON 17- THE QUALITY OF YOUR CONSCIOUSNESS AT THIS MOMENT IS WHAT SHAPES THE FUTURE, WHICH CAN ONLY BE EXPERIENCED AS THE NOW.

PRAYER: IN THIS PRESENT MOMENT, I EMBRACE GRATITUDE FOR ALL THAT I AM, ALL THAT I HAVE, AND ALL THAT I AM EXPERIENCING. I AM GRATEFUL FOR THE BREATH THAT FILLS MY LUNGS AND FOR THE MIRACULOUS EXISTENCE THAT IS UNFOLDING BEFORE ME.

Yoga Practice
The Warrior Pose III

How to do it

From Warrior I, hinge forward at the hips. Rest your abdomen on your front thigh. Step the back foot in and shift your weight into your front foot.

On an inhale, lift your back leg off the ground, straighten through the leg, and reach through your back heel. Press your palms together in front of your sternum (prayer hands) and gaze forward.

You can also place your arms along the hips, outstretched in front of you like you're flying, or on the floor underneath your shoulders.

The benefits

This heating pose strengthens your legs, outer hips, and upper back. It also helps improve balance and posture.

Morning Gratitude

Date: _______________

What is my main goal...

____

____

____

New a s sum ptio ns abou t mys elf?

____

____

____

3 things I'm grateful for today are...

____

____

____

"Happiness is a habit."

THE WAY OF THE ADVERSARY

18

**Verse-"Be sober, be vigilant; because your adversary the devil walks about like a roaring lion."
1Peter 5:8**

The greatest adversary you will face on your way to opulence is doubt. Doubt can be a powerful obstacle when it comes to manifesting your desires and achieving your goals. It acts as a barrier that prevents you from fully embracing the possibilities and potential outcomes that you desire. Doubt often arises as a result of fear of the unknown, not being in control, fear of failure, or skepticism about the principles of manifestation. All this is tied to your unbelief in the power within you, unbelief in the Father. You must understand that "of your own, you do nothing but the Father that dwelleth in you, He doeth the works". When you doubt, you send conflicting signals to your subconscious mind and your essential being. While consciously you may want to manifest something specific, your doubts create a dissonance that hinders the manifestation process. Your doubts become self-fulfilling prophecies, that is, you subconsciously sabotage your efforts and prevent the desired outcome from materializing. An unwavering belief in your ability to realize your desire aligns your thoughts, emotions, and actions with that intention. This alignment creates a powerful vibrational frequency that attracts the desired outcome into your life. Doubt disrupts this alignment. Instead of focusing on what you want, the adversary shifts your attention to what you lack or the potential obstacles that may stand in your way. Repeating your affirmations regularly is a very effective weapon to overcome the adversary.

LESSON 18- DOUBT IS THE ENEMY SEEKING TO STEAL, KILL, AND DESTROY YOUR DESIRES. HAVE FAITH IN THE POWER WITHIN YOU.

PRAYER: THANK YOU, FATHER, FOR YOUR PATIENCE AND GRACE. I SURRENDER MY DOUBTS TO YOU, KNOWING THAT YOU ARE GREATER THAN ANY UNCERTAINTY I MAY FACE.

Yoga Practice
Plow Pose

How to do it

Lie on your back with your arms by your sides and your legs extended.

Bend your knees and lift your legs, buttocks, and back all at once.

Bring your knees close to your forehead, and support your back with

your hands. Slowly straighten your legs and spine, reach the toes to

the floor, release the arms, squeeze the shoulder blades and interlace

your fingers.

Stay in plow pose for 30 seconds to 1 minute.

The benefits

Plow pose stretches the shoulders and back, calms the brain, and

helps release accumulated stress and tension. This pose also boosts

circulation, strengthens the upper body, and stimulates the immune

system.

Morning Gratitude

Date: _______________

What is my main goal...

____
____
____

New a s sum ptio ns abou t mys elf?

____
____
____

3 things I'm grateful for today are...

____
____
____

"Happiness is a habit."

THE WAY OF THE WILL
19

Verse-"A man without self-control is like a city broken into and left without walls." Proverbs 25:28

The Will is the power-control of your mind, it holds your thoughts in a singular given direction until a result has been accomplished. You cannot take action without a strong Will to do such said action. If you want to go to a certain place, without the Will to go there, you could not even start, nor could you retain the thought of the place long enough to arrive. You would start in the right direction, and then because there was no sustaining Will-Power in the thought, you might turn and go in another direction. It is the Will that holds the thought of a given purpose until it is accomplished or keeps an idea in its place in the mind until it is manifested in form. Your success or failure is dependent upon your mental control, and the Will is the controlling factor. Therefore, you must train and exercise your Will, because a weak Will cannot hold or control your thought power for a long duration. With a properly trained Will, you can pick up a thought at choice, hold it until it has finished its work, let it go, and then pick up another thought when you choose to. Without a strong Will, your imaginal act will become burdensome, you will have difficulty in holding a picture or scenario in your mind long enough to experience the feeling of the wish fulfilled. The Will exercise below will help strengthen your Will.

LESSON 19- THE MIND IS LIKE A STUBBORN BEAST; YOU NEED A STRONG WILL TO TAME IT.

PRAYER: I COME BEFORE YOU TODAY FATHER SEEKING GUIDANCE AND STRENGTH FOR A STRONG WILL. I RECOGNIZE THAT HAVING A STRONG WILL IS CRUCIAL IN OVERCOMING CHALLENGES AND PURSUING MY DREAMS. I HUMBLY ASK FOR YOUR SUPPORT AS I EMBARK ON THIS JOURNEY OF STRENGTHENING MY WILLPOWER.

WILL EXERCISE

Place a notebook and pencil by your side before beginning. Now take fifty matches, beads, buttons, bits of paper, or any other small objects, and drop them slowly and deliberately into a box one by one, with a feeling of contentment and satisfaction, declaring with each movement, "I will to will." The one and most important thought is that you are training your will for the particular advantage of having a trained will, and this is why you should cultivate the feeling of contentment. The only method by which you can study the development of your will is by self-analysis and introspection, so, when you have finished your practice, ask yourself such questions as these: "What did I think about the exercise while I was doing it? Did I believe it would cultivate my will, or did I do it just because I was told to? Did I concentrate on dropping the matches into the box, or was I more concerned with their arrangement, or was I distracted with other thoughts, good or bad? Was I watching the time impatiently, or was I consciously engaging in thoughts of satisfaction and contentment? Did I have a sense of strain, or did it brace me up? Do I believe that it will train my will if I faithfully follow it up long enough to prove it?" etc. Write down this series of questions and answers in your notebook. You will find it both interesting and encouraging to keep this record and thus watch your progress.

Morning Gratitude

Date: _______________________

What is my main goal...

____
____
____

Things i will start assuming about myself?

____
____
____

3 things I'm grateful for today are...

____
____
____

"Happiness is a habit."

THE WAY OF THE KINGDOM
20

Verse-"For indeed, the kingdom of God is within you." Luke 17:21

The Kingdom of God is not a physical place or a distant realm but a state of consciousness within each individual. In this kingdom, you are king and must operate from that knowledge to command your reality. "Except a man be born again, he cannot see the kingdom of God." That is; except you leave behind your present conception of yourself and assume the nature of the new birth, you will continue to out-picture your current limitations. "Seek ye first the kingdom of God, and his righteousness; and all these things shall be added unto you." The secret to altering your external surroundings is to become aware of the creative force that exists within you. You can't alter your circumstance by changing external things any more than you can change your reflection by shattering the mirror. "Whatever you bind on earth shall be bound in heaven, and whatever you loose on earth shall be loosed in heaven." Heaven, which is your subconscious mind, will enact that which your objective mind (earth) impresses upon it. Use the power of your imagination while maintaining a kingdom attitude, which entails being content and joyous on the inside, if you want to make your goal a reality. Manifesting from the Kingdom of God begins with aligning one's thoughts, beliefs, and intentions with the principles and values of the Kingdom. This involves cultivating qualities such as love, compassion, gratitude in all aspects of life. By embodying these principles, you create a harmonious resonance with the divine energy, allowing your desires to manifest in alignment with your current state of being.

LESSON 20- THE KINGDOM OF GOD IS NOT EATING AND DRINKING, BUT RIGHTEOUSNESS AND PEACE AND JOY IN THE HOLY SPIRIT.

PRAYER: AS I STRIVE FOR THE IMPLEMENTATION OF KINGDOM PRINCIPLES, HELP ME TO LIVE BY THE VALUES OF THE KINGDOM HERE AND NOW. FILL MY HEART WITH HUMILITY, AND KINDNESS.

Yoga Practice
The Triangle Pose

How to do it

Stand with feet wide, 3–4 feet apart. Shift your right heel out so your toes are pointing slightly inward. Turn your left foot out 90 degrees. Line up your left heel with the arch of your right foot.

Keeping both legs straight, ground through your feet. Lift arms into a T at shoulder height. Reach forward with your front arm. When you can't reach anymore, hinge at the front hip. Bring your front arm down to your shin, a foam block, or the ground. Lift your back arm up toward the sky and spread your fingers. Take your gaze down to the floor or up toward your lifted hand.

The benefits

While this pose can be challenging for those with tight muscles, it will help promote balance, stretch the hamstrings and inner thighs, and create a feeling of expansion in the body.

Morning Gratitude

Date: _______________________

What is my main goal...

____

____

____

Things i will start assuming about myself?

____

____

____

3 things I'm grateful for today are...

____

____

____

"Happiness is a habit."

THE WAY OF DETACHMENT

21

Verse-"Be anxious for nothing." Philippians 4:6

The way of detachment refers to your ability to let go of attachments and outcomes, freeing yourself from the limitations of the ego and embracing a state of inner peace and freedom. Detachment does not imply apathy or indifference toward your desires, on the contrary, it involves holding a strong belief in the reality of your imaginal acts and persistently assuming the feeling of the wish fulfilled. It is about releasing the need to control the outcome of your manifestation and allowing Divine intelligence to work out the means. It also involves releasing the need for immediate physical evidence or external validation of your desires. It means not being attached to the outcome or the specific way in which your desires will manifest. Detachment requires a disciplined and focused mind. It involves shifting your attention from the external world and its limitations into the realm of the Kingdom, where all possibilities exist. "As the heavens are higher than the earth, so are my ways higher than your ways and my thoughts than your thoughts".Step back after your imaginary act and let the Father do His work. On the canvas of your mind, the Father is like a painter, patiently waiting to produce a masterpiece. If you will stop thinking about how your goal will come to pass, you will be giving Him a blank canvas on which to begin painting. Believe in His efforts and "Let the Painter, Paint".

LESSON 21- DETACHMENT DOES NOT MEAN YOU DON'T OWN ANYTHING. IT MEANS THAT NOTHING OWNS YOU.

PRAYER: TEACH ME TO LET GO OF MY FEARS, WORRIES, AND ANXIETIES, FOR THEY BIND ME TO A LIMITED PERSPECTIVE AND PREVENT ME FROM EXPERIENCING THE BEAUTY OF THE PRESENT MOMENT.

Yoga Practice
Crow Pose

How to do it

Come down to a deep squat, with your feet a few inches apart and your heels lifted off the mat. Make your knees wider than your hips.

Bring your palms down in front of you between your knees, shoulder-width apart. Hook your shins around your upper arms.

Look forward, shift your weight forward onto your hands, and lift your feet off the floor. Pull up through your arms and abs, and round your upper back. If you can, bring your toes to touch beneath your tailbone.

The benefits

Crow Pose builds (and requires) serious strength in your arms, wrists, core, and hip flexors.

Morning Gratitude

Date: _______________

What is my main goal...

____

____

____

Things i will start assuming about myself?

____

____

____

3 things I'm grateful for today are...

____

____

____

"Happiness is a habit."

THE WAY OF REPETITION

22

Verse-"Pray without ceasing". 1 Thessalonians 5:17

Repetition can significantly enhance the effectiveness and efficiency of your manifestation process. Repetition helps reinforce your beliefs and intentions. When you are repeatedly focusing on a particular desire or goal, you are constantly reminding yourself of its importance and relevance in your life. By affirming and envisioning what you want regularly, you begin to align your conscious desires with your subconscious mind, strengthening your conviction in the power of manifestation. Your subconscious mind is a powerful force that influences your thoughts, emotions, and actions. Through repetition, you can program your subconscious mind to adopt new beliefs and thought patterns that are in alignment with your desired outcomes. By consistently affirming positive statements and visualizing success, you create new neural pathways and reinforce positive programming. Repetition helps to change and overcome limiting beliefs that may be blocking your manifestations. Often, deeply ingrained beliefs and past experiences can create doubts and self- sabotaging thoughts that hinder your progress. By repetitively affirming positive statements and visualizing success, you can gradually replace those limiting beliefs with empowering ones. Repetition allows you to shift your focus from what you perceive as limitations to what is possible, ultimately attracting the outcomes you seek into your reality.

LESSON 22- THROUGH REPETITION, YOU CAN PROGRAM YOUR SUBCONSCIOUS MIND TO ADOPT NEW BELIEFS.

PRAYER: IN THIS MOMENT OF PRAYER, I COME BEFORE YOU SEEKING YOUR GRACE AND GUIDANCE. I ASK FOR YOUR HELP IN CULTIVATING CONTINUITY IN MY LIFE AND REMAINING STEADFAST ON THE PATH YOU HAVE SET BEFORE ME.

Yoga Practice
Repeat Crow Pose

How to do it

Come down to a deep squat, with your feet a few inches apart and your heels lifted off the mat. Make your knees wider than your hips.

Bring your palms down in front of you between your knees, shoulder-width apart. Hook your shins around your upper arms.

Look forward, shift your weight forward onto your hands, and lift your feet off the floor. Pull up through your arms and abs, and round your upper back. If you can, bring your toes to touch beneath your tailbone.

Morning Gratitude

Date: _______________________

What is my main goal...

____
____
____

Things i will start assuming about myself?

____
____
____

3 things I'm grateful for today are...

____
____
____

"Happiness is a habit."

THE WAY OF CONVICTION

23

Verse-"If thou can believe, all things are possible to him that believeth." Mark 9:23

Conviction is a feeling of absolute certainty about what something Is or means to you without a doubt. It is a state of knowing. When you are certain about your beliefs, they become convictions. Beliefs create and beliefs destroy, they direct your life. It is not what you want that you attract, you attract what you believe to be true. When you have a strong conviction, it suggests you are confident in your ability to achieve your goals. In truth you are already that which you want to be, and your refusal to believe this is the only reason you do not see it in your reality. The world is yourself pushed out. Ask yourself what you want and then give it to yourself! Do not question how it will come about; just go your way with the conviction that the evidence of what you have done must appear, and it will. Learn to shake yourself loose from what the world believes is the only reality, rather believe in your ability to create a new reality.

It is said in the scriptures; "with God all things are possible". Another verse, states "All things are possible to him that believes". No Limit was placed on the ability of God the Father, but the only limit placed on man is in his ability to believe. "I will answer them before they call to me. While they are still talking about their needs, I will go ahead and answer their prayers". This is the promise made to those who believe and recognized the Father as the power within them. The promise operates by faith. If you believe, no effort is necessary to see the fulfillment of your every desire.

LESSON 23- IDENTIFY AND CHALLENGE LIMITING BELIEFS BY EXAMINING THEIR ORIGINS, EVIDENCE, AND LOGICAL VALIDITY.

PRAYER: DEAR FATHER, WITH UTMOST SINCERITY AND DEVOTION, I PRAY FOR A DEEPER AND UNWAVERING BELIEF. MAY MY FAITH CONTINUE TO GROW AND FLOURISH, NOURISHED BY THE DIVINE GRACE THAT SURROUNDS US.

Yoga Practice
Wheel Pose

How to do it

Lie faceup with knees bent, feet flat on the floor, like you're prepping for Bridge Pose. Position your feet parallel to one another, hip-distance apart, with heels under the knees.

On an inhale, bring your hands to the floor, framing your ears. Your fingers should be facing your heels.

On an exhale, press down on your hands and feet. Lift your hips and chest off the floor. Straighten your arms and lift through your shoulders.

To come out of the pose, bend your arms and slowly lower your upper back down to the floor.

The benefits

This backbend opens the entire front of the body. It strengthens the muscles in your back, shoulders, and hamstrings.

Morning Gratitude

Date: _______________

What is my main goal...

____
____
____

Things i will start assuming about myself?

____
____
____

3 things I'm grateful for today are...

____
____
____

"Happiness is a habit."

THE WAY OF PRAYER
24

Verse-"But when you pray, go into your room and shut the door and pray to your Father who is in secret." Matthew 6:6

Prayer is the art of believing what is denied by the senses or the conscious mind. You shut the door to your Conscious mind and commune with the Father, your Subconscious. The first requirement for a successful prayer is controlled thought and imagination. Vain repetition of words and begging is not prayer. It requires tranquility of mind. Prayer is done in secret; "and thy father which seeth in secret shall reward thee openly". The customary ceremonies used in prayers are mere superstitions. The results obtained from prayer are not just by faith alone, but faith with understanding. The Universal Law of Reversibility is the foundation on which answered prayers are based. For example, if heat can produce mechanical motion, so to mechanical motion can produce heat. If electricity can produce magnetism, then inversely magnetism can produce electrical current. Therefore, if your answered prayer awakens in you a certain feeling or emotion, then by the Law, if you can create such a feeling or emotion, it will inversely produce your answered prayer. This is why you were told to pray believing you already have what you prayed for. Praying is recognizing yourself to be that which you desire to be, rather than begging God for that which you desire. Awaken within you the feeling that you are and have that which you desire. The feeling of the wish fulfilled if sustained must objectify the state that created it. If a physical fact can produce a psychological state, then a psychological state can produce a physical fact.

LESSON 24- IF YOU PRAYER BELIEVING YOU ALREADY HAVE THE ANSWER, YOU WILL HAVE THE ANSWER TO MY PRAYERS

PRAYER: I HUMBLY COME BEFORE YOU TODAY, SEEKING YOUR GUIDANCE AND WISDOM AS I DESIRE TO LEARN HOW TO PRAY. YOU ARE THE SOURCE OF ALL KNOWLEDGE AND UNDERSTANDING, AND I TRUST IN YOUR LOVING PRESENCE AS I EMBARK ON THIS JOURNEY.

Yoga Practice

The Bridge Pose

How to do it

Lie faceup with knees bent, feet flat on the floor, and arms at your sides with palms facedown. Keep your feet parallel and hip-width apart, heels stacked under your knees.

On an inhale, activate through the legs and the glutes. Press the floor away with your feet and lift the hips off the floor toward the sky.

If your shoulders are tight and you want more leverage, try holding the sides of your yoga mat and lifting your hips. You may also wish to interlace your fingers underneath your "bridge" and shimmy your shoulders under the chest.

When you're ready to come down, lift your heels up and slowly lower your hips back to the ground, one vertebra at a time.

The benefits

This energizing backbend opens your chest and stretches your neck and spine. It can calm the mind, reduce anxiety, and help improve digestion.

Morning Gratitude

Date: ______________________

What is my main goal...

____

____

____

Things i will start assuming about myself?

____

____

____

3 things I'm grateful for today are...

____

____

____

"Happiness is a habit."

THE WAY OF SLUMBER

25

Verse-"In slumbering upon the bed; then He openeth the ears of men and sealeth their instruction." Job 33:16

You spend one-third of your stay on earth in slumber, for it is the natural door into the subconscious. It is in sleep that man enters the subconscious to make his impressions and receive his instructions. In slumber, the conscious and the subconscious are creatively joined. Whatever you have in your conscious mind as you go to sleep, is a measure of your reality in the waking world. So never go to sleep feeling discouraged or dissatisfied, and never sleep in the consciousness of failure, for your subconscious whose natural state is sleep, sees you as you believe yourself to be, whether it be good, bad, or indifferent, the subconscious will faithfully embody your belief and projects it in the waking world. Nothing stops you from realizing your desire except your failure to feel that you are already that which you wish to be before you retire to slumber. Your subconscious gives form to your desire only when you sleep feeling your wish fulfilled. While you slumber, you move from this realm of particles into a substantial reality of a dimensionally larger realm of possibilities. In this world, you are usually the servant of your vision rather than its master, but if you become conscious of your dream and are in control of the direction of your thoughts, the internal fantasy of the dream can be turned into an external reality, that is you can cause an effect in the waking world by conscious manipulation of your thoughts in this realm of infinite possibilities. This is how great masters call those things that are not as though they were.

LESSON 25- YOU ARE A POWERFUL MULTIDIMENSIONAL BEING, YOU EXPERIENCE MULTIPLE DIMENSION OF REALITY IN SLUMBER.

PRAYER: AS I SLUMBER, MAY I CARRY THE GIFTS OF MINDFULNESS AND INSIGHT INTO MY CONSCIOUS DAY AS I AWAKE, HELP ME REMEMBER THE MESSAGES AND SYMBOLS FROM MY DREAMS, AND EMPOWER ME TO APPLY THEIR WISDOM TO MY LIFE.

Yoga Practice
Side Plank Pose

How to do it

Start in Downward-Facing Dog. Turn onto the outer edge of your right foot, making sure that your right foot and right hand are in alignment. Stack your left foot on top of your right. Lengthen through the spine through the crown of your head. Once you're stable, lift your left hand up toward the sky. Press the floor away from you with the bottom hand.

The benefits

This pose strengthens your shoulders, upper back, and abdominals. It also promotes core and scapular stability.

Morning Gratitude

Date: _________________________

What w as my d ream last night   ...

____
____
____

What d o i th ik i t means ?

____
____
____

3 things I'm grateful for today are...

____
____
____

"Happiness is a habit."

THE WAY OF ABUNDANCE

26

Verse-"I have come that they may have life and have it more abundantly." John 10:10

The idea of abundance has long been coveted by people around the world. Yet, despite its desirability, many struggle to tap into the abundance that is already within us. The measure of a man's life is not in the things he possesses, but in the number of things he can use rightly. To have the fullness of life is to have all the things we are capable of using rightly. The purpose of God is that all should have life and have it more abundantly. Life finds expression through the use of things. God is the mind of creation and is in all and through all of creation. Therefore, your desire to express yourself through things is from the mind of God searching for more expression of life. There is no limit to God. Nature is an inexhaustible storehouse of riches. Its supplies will never run short. The creative energy is alive and always producing new forms. When all the gold and silver have been dug from the earth, if humans still need gold and silver for the advancement of their development more will be produced by this creative energy. There is positively abundant supply omnipresent, but the demand for it must be made before the Law of the Universe permits it to come into the expression and use of the individual. God desires to give you everything you want to have. The universe is friendly to your desire. Make up your mind that this is true. You are to create, not compete for what is already created. You do not have to covet the property of others. No one has anything of which you cannot have the same.

LESSON 26- THE STOREHOUSE OF THE KINGDOM IS INEXHAUSTIBLE, FEAR NOT FOR THE LORD SHALL SUPPLY ALL YOUR NEEDS.

PRAYER: I OPEN MY HEART TO THE INFINITE ABUNDANCE THAT SURROUNDS ME. I COME BEFORE YOU WITH GRATITUDE AND A DESIRE TO RECOGNIZE AND EMBRACE THE ABUNDANT BLESSINGS IN MY LIFE.

Yoga Practice
Boat Pose

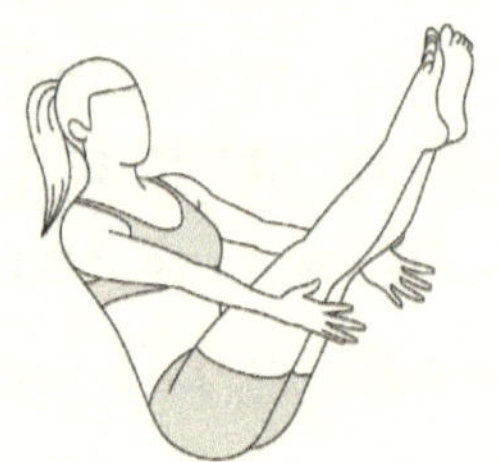

How to do it

Sit on the mat with your legs fully extended and lean your torso back.

Raise both legs to a 45-degree angle and reach your arms to the front, keeping them parallel to the floor.

Stay in boat pose for 30 seconds to 1 minute

The benefits

You will strengthen your abdominals and hip flexors.

Morning Gratitude

Date: _______________________

What is my main goal...

____

____

____

Things i will start assuming about myself?

____

____

____

3 things I'm grateful for today are...

____

____

____

"Happiness is a habit."

THE WAY OF GIVING

27

Verse-; "Each one must give as he has decided in his heart, not reluctantly or under compulsion, for God loves a cheerful giver." 2 Corinthians 9:7

Until now, everything we have talked about centered on what you want to have. Life is not one-sided, there is a give and a take, it is a two-way street. We must give back to the Father to show gratitude and faith in Him as our all-sufficient provider. In some religions, it is customary to give back a certain percentage (10%) of your income back to God. This practice eliminates greed and selfishness in you and increases your faith in the unlimited supply of the storehouse of the Father. "Prove me now herewith, saith the Lord of hosts, if I will not open you the windows of heaven, and pour you out a blessing, that there shall not be room enough to receive it."

Your giving is proof that you are grateful for all the good that comes to you, and it opens up more opportunities to receive from the Father. "One who is faithful in very little is also faithful in much, and one who is dishonest in very little is also dishonest in much". You must be faithful in giving back, it must be consistent, and you must give cheerfully. By giving to the Good Spiritual Work of Creation, you guarantee a continued partnership with the creator. Give to the Father where you feel you receive spiritual guidance and the effectiveness of your gift increases. If you are unsure where to send your gift, ask the Father and He will direct you. You do not need to belong to any religious institution. The idea is to send it where you feel it promotes the Spiritual Work of the creator and helps with your spiritual progress.

LESSON 27- GIVING IS A WAY OF SAYING THANK YOU WITH ACTION AND POSITIONING YOU TO RECEIVE MORE BLESSINGS.
PRAYER; I OFFER MY HEARTFELT GRATITUDE FOR THE ABUNDANCE IN MY LIFE AND FOR THE OPPORTUNITY TO GIVE. MAY MY PRAYERS BE HEARD AND ANSWERED, AND MAY I BE GUIDED TO GIVE WITH AN OPEN HEART.

Yoga Practice
Eagle Pose

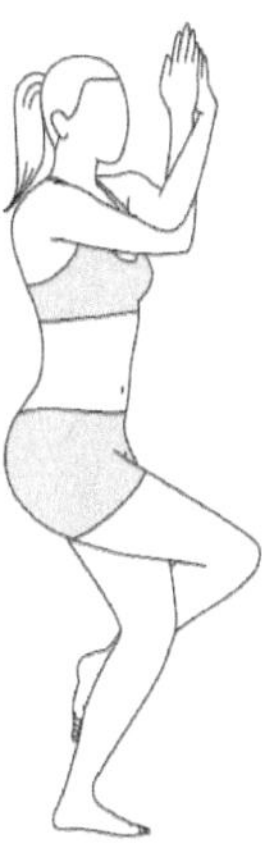

How to do it

Stand up straight, stretch your arms forward, open your back, and cross your left arm on top of the right. Bend your elbows, raise and cross your forearms, so that the palms of your hands are facing each other. Bend your knees and put your weight on the left foot. Pull your right knee toward the chest and then cross your right thigh over the left and hook the right foot behind the left calf.

Stay in eagle pose for 15 to 30 seconds and then repeat with the arms and legs reversed.

The benefits

The eagle pose helps to improve balance and increases your flexibility and strength. This pose helps to loosen the legs and hips and stretches the thighs, shoulders, and upper back.

Morning Gratitude

Date: _______________________

What is my main goal...

____
____
____

Things i will start assuming about myself?

____
____
____

3 things I'm grateful for today are...

____
____
____

"Happiness is a habit."

THE WAY OF FORGIVENESS
28

Verse-; "And whenever you stand praying, forgive, if you have anything against anyone." Mark 11:25

Forgiveness is not about condoning or forgetting the actions of others rather it is about freeing yourself from the emotional burden associated with those actions. To forgive means to choose to release another from the perception you have been projecting upon them. It is, therefore, an act of forgiving yourself of your projections. Harboring negative emotions towards others ultimately harms you. By choosing forgiveness, you reclaim your power and take control of your emotional well-being. Your linear perception of things is so very limited. The judgments you make are so often clouded and incorrect. Sometimes other people have purposely hurt you, other times you might have misjudged a situation.

You should also learn to forgive yourself for past mistakes and guilt. Self- forgiveness is an essential aspect of personal growth, as it enables you to let go of self-imposed limitations and embrace your inherent worthiness. Be kind to yourself, acknowledge your imperfections, and realize you are on a journey to perfection, learn from past experiences without dwelling on them. Forgiveness is not a one-time event but a continuous practice. It requires a willingness to let go, cultivate empathy, and choose love over resentment. By forgiving others and yourself, you create a positive environment for your desire to manifest in your reality, and also improve harmonious relationships with others, and hence a more fulfilling life.

LESSON 28- LEARN TO FORGIVE YOURSELF FIRST BEFORE YOU CAN WHOLEHEARTEDLY FORGIVE OTHERS.

PRAYER: GRACIOUS FATHER, TEACH ME TO EXTEND THE SAME FORGIVENESS AND COMPASSION TO OTHERS WHO HAVE WRONGED ME. GRANT ME THE ABILITY TO LET GO OF RESENTMENT, BITTERNESS, AND THE DESIRE FOR REVENGE.

Yoga Practice
Full Side Plank Pose

How to do it

Start in a side plank pose, with your left foot and leg on top of the

right. Lift your left leg up and grab your big toe with your left hand.

Stay in extended side plank for 30 seconds, return to side plank pose

and then repeat on the opposite side.

Maintain the hips high, plant your right hand and foot firmly on the

floor and roll your right shoulder back. Gaze at your left foot and keep

both legs straight.

The benefits

The full side plank pose strengthens the wrists, arms, shoulders, core,

and legs and stretches the hips and hamstrings. This yoga pose also

helps to improve balance and stability, relieves tension, and prevents

lower back pain.

Morning Gratitude

Date: _______________________

What is my main goal...

Things i will start assuming about myself?

3 things I'm grateful for today are...

"Happiness is a habit."

THE WAY OF GRATITUDE

29

Verse-; "Giving thanks always for all things unto God and the Father." Ephesians 5:20

Gratitude is a process of mental adjustment and attunement. It brings you closer to the source of your supply. Having received one gift from the Father, most people cut the wires which connect them with Him by failing to make acknowledgment and showing profound gratitude. The nearer you are to the source of your wealth, the more wealth you shall receive. Gratitude alone can keep you looking towards the infinite storehouse of the father and prevent you from thinking that supply is limited. The Father responds with an immediate movement toward you when you extend your mind in gratitude and thanks to the Creative Power. This is because it involves an expenditure of force. "Draw nigh unto God, and He will draw nigh unto you." If your gratitude is strong and constant, your supply from the Father will be strong and continuous. You cannot exercise much power over your current reality without gratitude, because it is gratitude that keeps you connected with power. The grateful mind is always fixed upon the best. Therefore, it draws the best things to itself. Do not rage against corrupt politicians and other captains of industry instead acknowledge that the Father is using them in the meantime to arrange the lines of transmission along which your riches will come to you.

It is necessary to cultivate the habit of being grateful for everything that comes to you because all things are working together for your good.

LESSON 29- ACKNOWLEDGING THE GOOD THAT YOU ALREADY HAVE IN YOUR LIFE IS THE FOUNDATION FOR ALL ABUNDANCE.

PRAYER: I COME BEFORE YOU WITH A HEART FULL OF GRATITUDE AND APPRECIATION. I RECOGNIZE THE COUNTLESS BLESSINGS AND ABUNDANT GIFTS YOU HAVE BESTOWED UPON ME. I AM HUMBLED BY YOUR GRACE AND LOVE FOR ME.

Yoga Practice
Happy Baby Pose

How to do it

Lie on your back, exhale, and bend your knees into the belly. Inhale and hold the outside edge of your feet. Open your knees and bring them up toward your armpits. Hold the pose for 30 seconds to 1 minute.

The benefits

The happy baby pose lengthens the spine, releases tension in the lower back, opens the hips and the inner thighs, and stretches the hamstrings. This pose also helps to relieve stress and fatigue and calms the brain.

Morning Gratitude

Date: _______________________

What is my main goal today...

____

____

____

3 People I'm grateful for today are...

____

____

____

3 things I'm grateful for today are...

____

____

____

"Happiness is a habit."

DAY THIRTY
THE WAY OF LOVE
30

Verse-; "God is love, and all who live in love live in God, and God lives in them." 1 John 4:16

Love is the only thing that matters in this world. It is not merely an emotion or feeling experienced by humans, but rather a fundamental creative force that permeates the entire cosmos. The Universe originated from a divine impulse of love, which is referred to as "creative energy." This creative energy is an intelligent force, guided by love, which brought all things into existence. Love is not only a passive force, but an active, transformative power. It can heal, restore, and unite. Love, when expressed and experienced by individuals, have the potential to harmonize relationships, foster compassion, and bring about a higher state of consciousness. It is at this state of consciousness that your heart desires quickly come into existence. A life without love would be worthless. You could live without a car or go on vacation, but could you live without love in your life? Love is the motivating force behind our desires and aspirations. It propelled us to seek growth, development, and connection with others. It is the driving factor behind our creative endeavors and the manifestation of our dreams and goals. More love for yourself always precedes the ability to love others. Start talking to yourself like a best friend and compliment yourself on all your special qualities. Love is truly magical and has a power all of its own; just like a snowball will add size as it rolls down the mountain, so too will love gather the strength to push aside all obstacles in your life.

LESSON 30- THE FOUNDATION OF ANY HEALTHY AND LOVING RELATIONSHIP BEGINS WITH SELF-LOVE. EMBRACE AND ACCEPT YOURSELF AS YOU ARE, WITH ALL YOUR STRENGTHS, WEAKNESSES, AND IMPERFECTIONS.

PRAYER: DIVINE SOURCE OF LOVE, I SURRENDER MYSELF TO THE POWER OF LOVE. FILL MY HEART WITH YOUR UNCONDITIONAL LOVE, SO THAT I MAY RADIATE IT OUTWARDS, TOUCHING THE LIVES OF ALL THOSE I ENCOUNTER.

Yoga Practice
The Goddess Pose

How to do it

Start in mountain pose and, as you exhale, step your feet wide apart and lift your arms to shoulder height. Rotate your feet out to the sides, bend your elbows, and turn the palms facing each other. Exhale as you bend your knees and squat down. Stay in goddess pose for 30 seconds to 1 minute.

The benefits

The goddess pose strengthens the thighs, glutes, core, and shoulders, boosts circulation, and opens the hips, groins, and chest.

Morning Gratitude

Date: ____________________

People I am sending Love to...

____

____

____

I will spread Love today by..

____

____

____

3 things I'm grateful for today are...

____

____

____

"Happiness is a habit."

Conclusion

In conclusion, "The Way of Opulence" serves as an enlightening guide that transcends mere financial prosperity to delve into the profound art of living abundantly. Throughout its pages, readers have journeyed alongside the author's insightful exploration of the multifaceted pathways that lead to opulence—embracing not only material wealth but also the riches of self-awareness, meaningful connections, and a purpose-driven existence.

The book's wisdom has illuminated the intricate interplay between mindset and action, illustrating how cultivating a mindset of abundance can ignite a cascade of transformative actions that shape destinies. It reminds us that true opulence arises from the fusion of gratitude, conscious decision-making, and an unwavering commitment to personal growth.

With every chapter, "The Way of Opulence" has encouraged us to release limiting beliefs, challenging us to expand our notions of what is possible. The author's adept storytelling and relatable anecdotes have made the journey both engaging and relatable, providing readers with relatable touchpoints to anchor their pursuit of opulence.

As we bid farewell to these pages, let us carry forth the profound insights gained from this book, may its teachings continue to inspire us to embrace abundance in all its forms, to foster a life of fulfillment, and to contribute positively to the world around us. In our ongoing pursuit of opulence, may we never lose sight of the fact that the truest wealth lies not only in what we possess but in the richness within us.

Write Your Testimony

i am grateful